Miscellaneous Meanderings

It's pouring out heart' s content sour and sweet

Dr. Snigdha Jha

India | USA | UK

Made with ❤ on the BookLeaf Publishing Platform
www.bookleafpub.in
www.bookleafpub.com

Dedication

Dedicated in memory of my loving Dad. Papa you left too soon. Wish you could have stayed a little longer. How unkind and cruel God was to snatch you in the midst of us. Without you life sucks but still cannot say yuck. Because your loving grandson is my responsibility, and I will unite with you finally in Heaven only when I pass all the traits and human values you instilled in us so lovingly

Preface

The book Miscellaneous Meanderings is an outcome of moments both sombre and gay. It comprises poems written on a variety of issues and themes. My 70-year-old father's untimely demise has almost shaken me. The loss I know can never be replenished but yes, through written words, I have tried to come to terms with the loss. My father was my greatest asset, first male friend,philosophy, er and guide.3 poems of this anthology are written about him, the human par excellence that he was. In fact the book was started on his first death Anniversary and very first poem bears testimony to this fact.Two other poems eulogising his personality and persona were written when he was present with us in flesh and blood .In addition to it there are miscellaneous themes ranging from love , love for only child, women's emancipation related issues and all.Overall it's a tapestry of varied and varying emotions

Acknowledgements

This book ""Miscellaneous Meanderings " is a cathartic expression of emotions buried deep into the abyss of mind,body and soul.I have been writing poetry eversince my kindergarten days but major stint happened after submission of my PhD thesis on famous writer Namita Gokhale.So first and foremost I am indebted to my parents for incorporating in me literary leanings.My father himself being a technocrat never compelled me to go for technical education and reposed full trust in me for choosing subject of my choice.Though my score in science too was good but still I was never pressurised.My mother herself being an academician and literary tycoon instilled in me a love for classics in all languages.My maternal great grandfather was a scholar of English and Sanskrit and first graduate of his village of preindependent India.Luckily he stayed nearby till his dying days.Every evening he gave us a discourse on Oriental and occidental classics and motivated us to extent unknown.My teachers at school, college , university too motivated me to make literature my vocation.I owe all of them a gratitude laden heart.My poetic outburst happened after submission of my thesis so I owe gratitude to famous writer Namita Gokhale too.It would be sheer ingratitude if I fail to extend my thankfulness to my loving husband and only child.My husband's contribution in making me a poet is manifold and cannot be expressed in mere words .

An Ode to my Father in Heaven

An Ode to my Father in heaven

I never imagined
Not even in my
Worst nightmares
A day would come
Dear Pa
When I would be using
The past tense of verb
For your addressal
The dreaded disease
Appeared in it's last
Corrosive stage
And like a whirlwind
Snatched you in midst
Of all your loving
Relatives and friends
For two months
After diagnosis

There was a tussle
Between you and your
Entire family
For everyone knew the truth
That you won't live long
But they keep duping you
That it's a minor ailment
Little knowing that you are
Aware of the fact
That this disease won't let you
Live with us
Today it's an year
After your demise
But wound in my heart is
As fresh as new
You were a human par excellence
A God loving man
With utmost respect for
Seniors and infinite love
For juniors
You never discriminated
Between your family and
Wife' s and so there is
Not even a single person
In my maternal side too
Whose eyes fails to water
At a mere mention

Of your name sublime
You hold the trophy of being
The best son,son in law
Husband and father
To be precise
I sometimes wonder
From where you got
This quality

On your first Death
Anniversary
I pay you my heart 's tribute
With blood stained tears
O'my beloved dead
Father distant
Please keep us blessing
From Heaven High

Teddy her True Companion

1 Teddy her true companion

Born only was "She" to suffer
At the hands of her
Close relatives
Near and dear ones
An unwanted child
That's what they call her
Came to earth only because
The doctor rejected
The proposal of another
Abortion
Which the fragile mother
Already had three
As a punishment for bearing Daughters
That too in continous succession

A son was all what they wanted
Who would carry forward their
Renowned and trusted lineage

Daughters they consider a liability
Whose birth is akin to calamity
Who is someone else's commodity
So should be brought up in depravity
She being the fourth daughter
Was therefore always treated
With undue wrath and ire
Ignored, unloved and uncared
She was confined to the segregated corner
Of that huge household
With teddy by her side

Teddy was all she had
On whom she could bank upon
Whenever she was reprimanded
Without any obvious faults of her
She shed silent tears
Hugging teddy closer to her bosom
It was a safety blanket for her
For small animals dared never harm her
Considering teddy her adult superviser
Together they were since her birth
And she loved it very much

May God bless her with a loving mate
Who would change her wretched fate
Inseparable they should be In

Sunshine and rain
Happiness and pain
Thus ushering her to a
New better world
Of peace, joy and prosperity

A strong Resolve

A strong resolve

My dying pen
Lying segregated
In some distant
Dilapidated corner
Of my household
Required refinement
And polishing
For people,place and
Patriarchy compelled
Me to either
Take a break or
Quit writing
For the vile , vicious
And sordid relatives
Cum critics have tried
To infer the pain, struggle
And chaos of my
Female protagonists

As something personal
Profane
A useless lamentation
And disgrace

I kept myself off
From my writing
Pedestal
Dying inwardly
With unexpressed
Grief
However after
A month or two
Good sense
Prevailed and I
Took a vow
Never to abstain
Myself from
Writing which
Is not only my
Passion but elixir
If in my writings and
Teaching I profess
To break the boundaries
Why should I care
For the critics
Some of whom

Just delight in my
Imaginary imperfections
It's a social service
I am doing
For giving them moments
Of laughter and the like
So o dear ones
I am not going to
Change either.my style
Or stand
I shall keep writing
What I observe and
Find right
You are free to call
It a melancholic
Outburst

Apocalypse

Apocalypse

What type of civilisation
Are we heading towards
Where goodness has lost
It's essence
Vileness, sordidness and
Treachery have become
Quite rampant and
Simplicity, soberness and
Truthfulness are ridiculed
With Gusto unmatched
The age of surfaces it is
Having optimum thrust on
Appearences and ostentation
Whosoever dupes his partner
Is rewarded with unflinching
Dedication and devotion
Whereas those true ones

Gets violence ,tortures and
Traumas in return
Why is there such a
Subversion of values
Or whatever has been
Preached through
Time immemorial
Requires some
Serious modification
Bad is the new good
So henceforth
Do we require to
Redefine the truth

Or is it a sign
Of impending
Apocalypse
A devastation of magnitude
Infinite
Is required to bring forth
A new better developed
World
Where goodness prevails
And vileness is pushed
To dungeons clandestine

Hope

Hope

Born out of
A mother who is
In extreme pains
Of body and mind
Hope tries to
Get delivered
As early as possible
To relieve it's
Mother of excruciating
Pain.
But no it's delivery
Is not as easy as one expects
It to be
Failure and rejections
It's two deadly
Foes tries to
Aid in it's abortion
So that it's existence

Is lost forever and
They reign supreme
Pushing the mother
Into deep dungeons
Of agony and despair
But alas that Hope
Is a fighter and it doesn't
Allow anyone to
Supersede
Fighting endlessly
It finally succeds in
Overcoming all
Failures and despair
Thus filling everyone
Lives with mirth and
Gaity
Let's all hail the
Hope and pray that
It continues it's
Presence
In our lives
So that it brightens
Each of our
Gloomy nights

Writing

Writing

A cathartic balm
Soul's cry hidden from
All is writing
When no one understands
Your pain ,fear,and
Guilt
The pen and paper becomes
Your mate
The pen drenching all
Your skirmishes of mind
And body into paper
Which absorbs silently
Without ridiculing or exhibiting
It infront of this bad mad
Cruel world

In between those horrible
Nights

When no one is there
To rock you to sleep
Or fondle your tresses
Like loving and adorable
Grandmother
Don't cry or panic
Instead open your pen
Or keyboard and start
Scribbling whatever comes
Into your tortured mind and
Soul
After some uncouth moments
Or time
You will feel the lightness
Engulfing you from
Within and feel
Relaxed even without the use
Of a painkiller or tranquilliser

Modern Savitri

Modern Savitri

Married she was
To an addict
Whose repeated
Failures and rejections
In life
Compelled him to
Take resort in
Drugs and wine
Plus he lost his
Parents at an age
Where a child
Needs guidance
The most
Unable to bear
Their loss
Love, affection and
Protectiveness
He daily started his day

With a quarter
Of rum or scotch

The routine continued
For years more than
Ten
Until one day
He married her
She being matured
And affectionate
Took hold of the
Situation
In a very
Chronological
Way
It was impossible
For him
To get rid of this
Bad habit
In one single day
So she made a plan
And implored him
To first lessen
The amount and
Then go for
Complete
Abstenance

She was nearing
The victory point
When all of a sudden
He was diagnosed
With liver ailments
The remedy of
Which lied in
Replacing the
Diseased one
With a healthier
One
The condition was
Critical and he
Himself with folded
Hands implored her
To let him go
But she was admant
And kept on murmuring
The words
You have to live to
Full
Not only for me
But for the child
You bore me

The task was tough

But she had a
Determination
Tougher than
Iron or steel
So she not only
Arranged everything
Singlehandedly
But also donated a part
Of her healthy liver
For mutual
Transplantation

Finally the man
Her man was
Brought alive from the
Cruel clutches
Of death and
The like
Isn't her story
Reminds you
Of legendary
Savitri and Satyavan
And can't we
Label her as
Savitri of
Today

In praise of my dynamic father

In praise of My Dynamic Father

My father stands tall
Resolute and unparalleled
In a world predominated
By hypocrisy and pretensions
An eldest son of a huge family
He was overburdened with
Responsibilities and liabilities

Simpleton that he was
He however never even twitched
His eyebrow
A father figure for his siblings
He did everything worthwhile
For their betterment
Most of them reciprocate his
Selfless love and service
Through their behaviour

Whosoever nurse grievances
Or abuse him
Also holds a place
In his heart
Forgiveness is a trait
He not only preaches
But also practice it with
A vigour unheard

A true devotee
Of Goddess Durga
He is quite against fake
Religiosity
And ostentation
A practitioner of women's
Equality
He paid same respect
To his
In laws as that of his
Parents

He is an adorable father
For his kids
Who worked tirelessly
In spite of illness
So that his daughters
And son lead a life

Of comfort
Sans penury, tears and
Unhappiness

May God always
Keep him healthy
And agile
So that he inculcates
Benevolence and generosity
In his future generations

Love

Love

What is love ?
Is it the one ?
A boyfriend feels for
His girlfriend whom
He has conquered
After scores of
Rejection
Or is it the one
A husband feels
For his wife
Only after a year
Or two of their
Wedding
But subsides once
The wife becomes
Pregnant and consequently
Hampers her figure
With repeated childbirths

No, no ,no
That love is
Not love but
Mere infatuation
Where bodily pleasures
And attractions
Plays a pivotal
Role

Infact truest love
Is something
That a young
Beautiful woman
Does have for her
Diseased deformed
Husband
Who shows no
Signs of improvement
Yet she serves him
With a hope that
He would get well
Soon
Similarly the old
Man who fondly
Cares for his
Paralytic wife

Without any
Irritation or
Turmoil

Love is not the
One that is bonded
By looks, hierarchy and
Family status quo
But the one
That survives
Even in unfavourable
Situations
If you truly love
A person from
Heart's deepest
Pores
Don't abondon him
When things are
Not right
Only then can
You evolve as
Loving luminaries
Of magnitudes
Infinite heights

Mind in turmoil

Mind in turmoil

His mind is a cacophony
Of surreal images
Disjointed thoughts
Come and go
In fragments
Making his existence
Stiffling
Yes for the first time
Alas! For the very first time
Is he unable to
Articulate his feelings
Pen down his
Thoughts
The grief stands tall
Like the blocks near
His typewriter
He is unable to move
How can God do this

To him

The elixir of his life
The inspiration of his
Dreams
His beloved
Loving adorable wife
Is dead
And he is
Condemned to live
A life
Worse than death

In temporal fits
Of pure schizophrenia
He yells vociferously
Give her back
Give her back
Or take me in
O proclaimed creator
People call you a saviour
But you are a monster
To call such a young
Pious and kind soul
So early
Was not an act of
Chivalry

But purely demonic and
Beastly

Nostalgia

Nostalgia

A time machine of
Magnitude infinite
Should be my vehicle
To carry me backwards
Into my own long lost
Childhood
When I was just a little
Girl
Having infinite curls
With grand and great grand
Parents at my side
I had the monopoly to do
Whatever I desire

The days were golden
And nights silver
without a care in the world
The childhood passed swiftly

With sweetest of memories
To recapitulate

Teenage and adulthood
Had their own merriment
And Strifes
But none could rival the
Joy of that Holi toy
For which we waited
For months in advance
Or that Diwali cracker
The glimpse of which
Compelled us to dance
With hairs crampled
Millions of expensive gadgets
Could not give the same joy
Nor hordes of diamonds
And gold ornaments
In tandem

Wish those days to come back
At least once
Where I would again be
The Queen of my house
An apple of parents and
Grand parents eyes
No tears or mental tensions

To bog me down
And no negative people
To demoralise and devastate
My existence and
Entity

Wicked women

Wicked women

Wicked women are
Made of stuff unknown
How much hard you try
They are not ready to
Mend their ways
Backbiting is their favourite
Pastime
It gives them a pleasure
Unknown

They are a black spot
On humanity in general
And womanhood in
Particular
Lacking wholly in looks
And intellect
They vociferously abuse
All those who possess

These in abundance
And in retaliation
Go on endlessly
Praising themselves
A great threat to
Women's emancipation
Movement
They are harbingers of
Unrest and conflicts
With their myopic vision
And narrow outlook
They are responsible for
Pushing women race
On the brink of devastation
And chaos

Honest Confession

Often have I wondered
To answer one simple
Question
What importance does
Writing and pen
Holds in my life
Is it just a soothing
Balm to provide
Cathartic effects ?
At times when days are sombre
And quiet
Many have criticised
My might to glorify
Tragedy and the
Like

It's true my dear
Friends that I have the capacity
To paint melancholy
On canvass made of

Bombastic words and
Decorative phrase
But believe me
Those sadness are
Not a part of my
Own life
In fact I at times
Gets so much bogged
By other 's tears and
Sighs
That writing appears to
Be the saviour
To take me out
From dungeons
Of depression
Thus I write to calm my
Own aching nerves and
Showcase other's exploitations
In front of the whole
Varied world

A promise to my Love

A promise to My Love

O ' my love
I don't know
Why I love you
So much
With you by my side
Life feels like heaven
On ride
Without you in domain
Everything appears
Sinister and profane
You are my goddess
You are my luck and
Every good happens
Only in your presence
Misfortunes and
Calamities struck me
Only when you are not around
For no harm can befall

A person
Who is flanked by
A soul so benevolent

Yet I don't know
Why at times
I hurt you and
Become a cause of
Your sorrows and
Depression
It rips my heart
To see your tears
Coming out of
Extreme Exasperation

I love you so much
That I cannot tolerate
Even Fleeting moments
Of ignorance and separation
So henceforth I I shall
Live live life on my
Terms
Without further delay
I make loving you
My vocation
And I promise to
Keep you happy

In all situations
Sweet or sour
To be precise

Sacrifice

Sacrifice

Has it ever occurred
To you ?
Why inspite of being
Weaker than many
Mighty ferocious beasts
We human beings are
On top of the evolution
Tree
When born we cannot
Stand or walk on feet
For more than a year
Or little less
Still we grow
Supreme and superior
Our thinking ability and
Ability to sacrifice
Distinguishes us from the
Rest .

Our mortal existence and
Unhurdled growth
Is a byproduct of our
Mother's sacrifice
Who sacrifices her food, sleep and
Career
For our bright future
Our Army men sacrifice
Of their lives
Allows us to live in an
Environment which is
Free and without undue
Negative vibes

But sacrifice should not be
Of Weak birds or beasts
For appeasing your deities
If you want to sacrifice
For achievement of some
Greater device
Sacrifice your lower desires
Love, lust, anger and attachment
Enhancing your soul's
Betterment
You would then emerge

As a spiritually awakened
Individual

Unnamed Relationship

Unnamed relationship

Snap the ties
Break the bonds
And go for a burial
Of all those relations
Which makes your existence
Painful
Allured by a tapestry of
Selfish motives
They go on hurting your
Sentiments
Now it's your turn
To show indifference
No matter whether they are
Connected by blood, love
Kinship or sex
Just throw their memories
Out of your precious lives

A true relationship
Is Unique and dignified
It doesn't require a name
For it's growth and sustenance
Spontaneously is it born
And takes a beautiful form
Slowly it becomes a
Part and parcel
Of your mortal existence
Absolute trust and
Pure love are it's vital
Nutrients
It helps you to
Come out of society's set
Preposition
And thus have redemption

19.

Sunshine of My Life

Sunshine of my life

Sunshine of my life are
You
Without whom I cease to
Be
My only child your absence
Appears to be tearing
My flesh and soul
With a pain invisible and
Free
Mornings are same and so
Are the evenings with breeze
Lovely and gay
But without you the freshness
Is gone and
Staleness pervades
Gnawing my heart and
Corroding my existence
With melancholy grey

Peacocks too come and
Appear to be addressing you
With their voice
Scathing and coarse
The place has lost It's charm
And so has the house
Started resembling with a
Graveyard
With a silence eerie and
Dreadful

You are the only good
Thing life ever gave me
Since the day of your
Conceivement
I am dressed in ethereal
Light of joy
Thanking Almighty
Profusely
I have forgiven him of
All the misfortunes and
Injustices he meted out
On me since time
Infinity
With every breath every
Batting of my eyelid

I miss you like hell
There cannot be any
Life for me
Without you in vicinity

You might have enough
Engagements to keep
You away from thoughts
Of your Mumma
But for me you are
My world
My elixir and panacea
Without which life
Is nothing but an
Amalgamation of horrendous
Cries, shrieks and yells

Mother's Instinct

Mother's Instinct

Telepathy she calls
Her power to know
When I am either
Highly ecstatic or
Deeply sombre
Is deeply perturbed
Even when we are
Afflicted with slightest of
Pain, trauma or tortures

Reigning supremely and
Superbly in
Unmatched wit, humour and
Intellect
My mother sacrificed her
Glittering career for a
Better upbringing of her
Children

Born in succession
Continuous

Working tirelessly
Day in and day
Out
She tried to inculcate
Values
In all her three children
And laid thrust on
Importance
Of sharing and
Caring
She had tried hard to let
Us evolve as a
Better human being
First and successful
Career professionals
Later

Though each day is
Dedicated in singing paens
In glory of her
Existence
On this special day
We all three siblings
In unison

Wish her the life's
Very best once and
Always henceforth

Transience

Transience

Love, laughter and
Happiness have
Limited validity
So are the tears
Which explodes
Spontaneously
Out of
Extreme melancholy
If both sadness and
Happiness are so
Transient
Why then do we
Become highly
Ecstatic when inundated
With pleasures and
Deeply sombre
When grief stricken

How happy we feel
When loved ones
Comes to meet
However it rips our
Hearts when
They depart
Nothing is permanent
Neither their stay
Nor is their
Departure
So we should
Always remain the
Same
Both in pleasures and
Pain
Infatuation with
Mortal beings is
Just a misnomer
As it can lead to
devastation
Attachment is lethal
For your soul's
Progression
So it's good to
Maintain a poise
In all circumstances
Precise

Only then Can you
Achieve a salvation
Both supreme and
Sublime

Missing my children's naughtiness

Missing my children 's naughtiness

Uncrumpled is the sheet
Kitchen is so neat
Not a trace of dust
Is there nor can you
Find rubbish lying
Here and there
Every toy is ordered
With all it's parts unbroken
Gone is the sound of laughter
Yellings and cries
What remains is the
Sound of my broken heart
Crying horrendously
Remembering my nephew and
Niece so dear
The house appers resplendent
But biting my soul with

A silence so scathing and
Dry
Cleanliness is next to
Godliness
But at times disorder, cacophony
Is also necessary as
It adds variety
To life 's melancholy
Brightness on a mischievous
Child 's face is worth all
The mess and nastiness
Children are carved in God's
Image so
We should enjoy all
Their naughtiness
With a heart clear and concise

Monsoon

Monsoon

Eulogised by many
For opulence of
Widespread beauty
Moonsoon indeed is.
A month of merriment
And celebrations
Overflowing with an
Opulence of vegetation
Earth is a green
Bedspread
Of abundance and .
Prosperity

A great reliever
From unbearable
Heat
It is a welcome relief

However it also is
Tormenting
For those who are separated
From their love
Monsoon invokes in them......
A deep yearning
Thus making their existence
Stiffling

He

He

He is a bitter potion
Or medicine
Whose worth cannot be
Appreciated as a child
But only when maturity
Dawns on our foolish
Heads

Ordained by inevitable
Fate
He is destined to be
My
Invincible mate
The inspiration of my
Latent desires and
Dreams
He propels me to move
Forward

Pretending to be callous
He harbours deepest concerns

Obsessively possessive
And vitriolic at times
He is blessed with
An all pervading
Enigma, and is a tough
Nut to crack

It's a blessing to
Have him as a life partner
Who augment me towards correspondence
With my sole creator
And thus achieve supreme
Unrivalled pleasure